This book belongs to:

Draw & Color Insects & Bugs

Coloring Book

Mary Lou Brown
Sandy Mahony

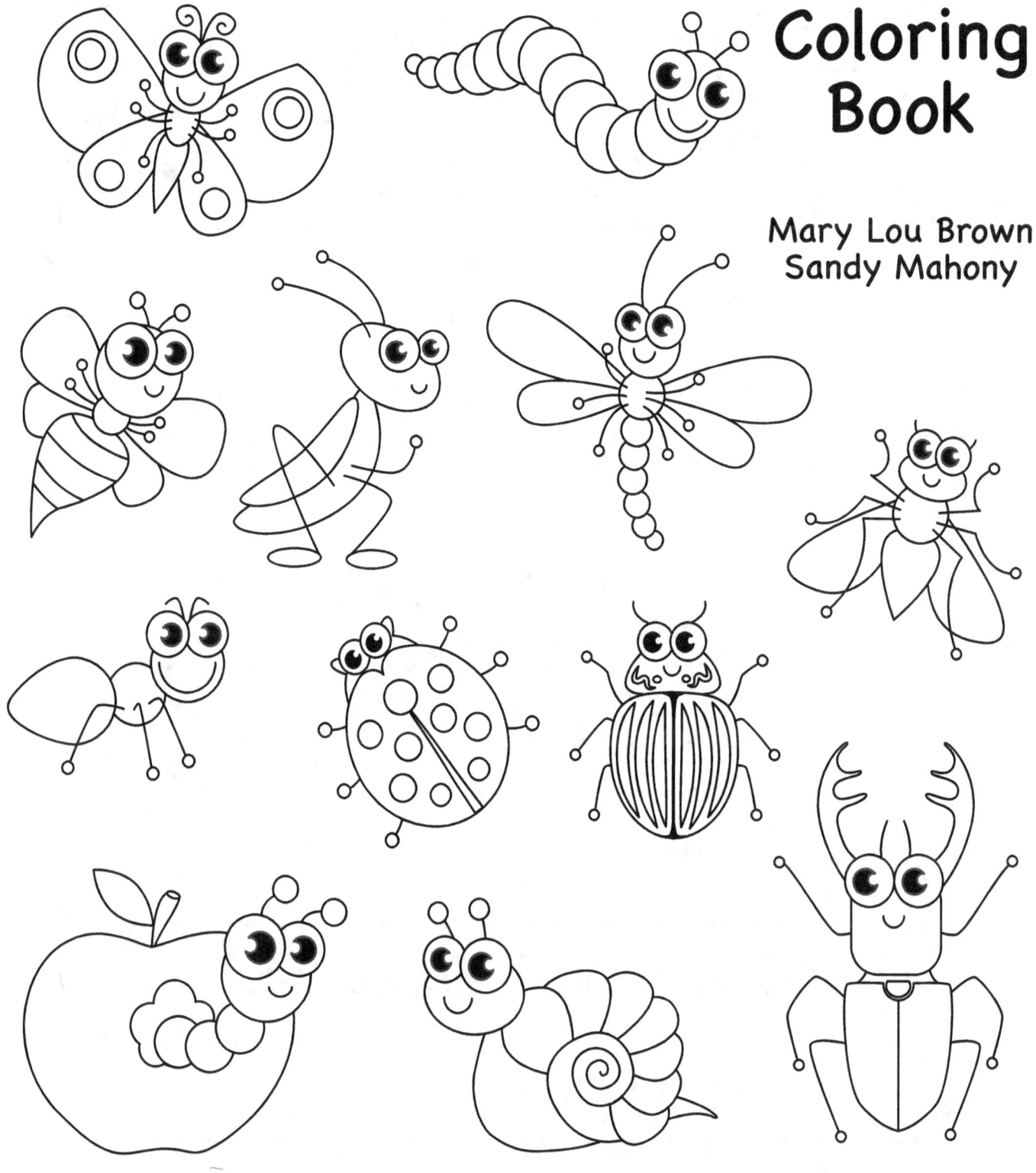

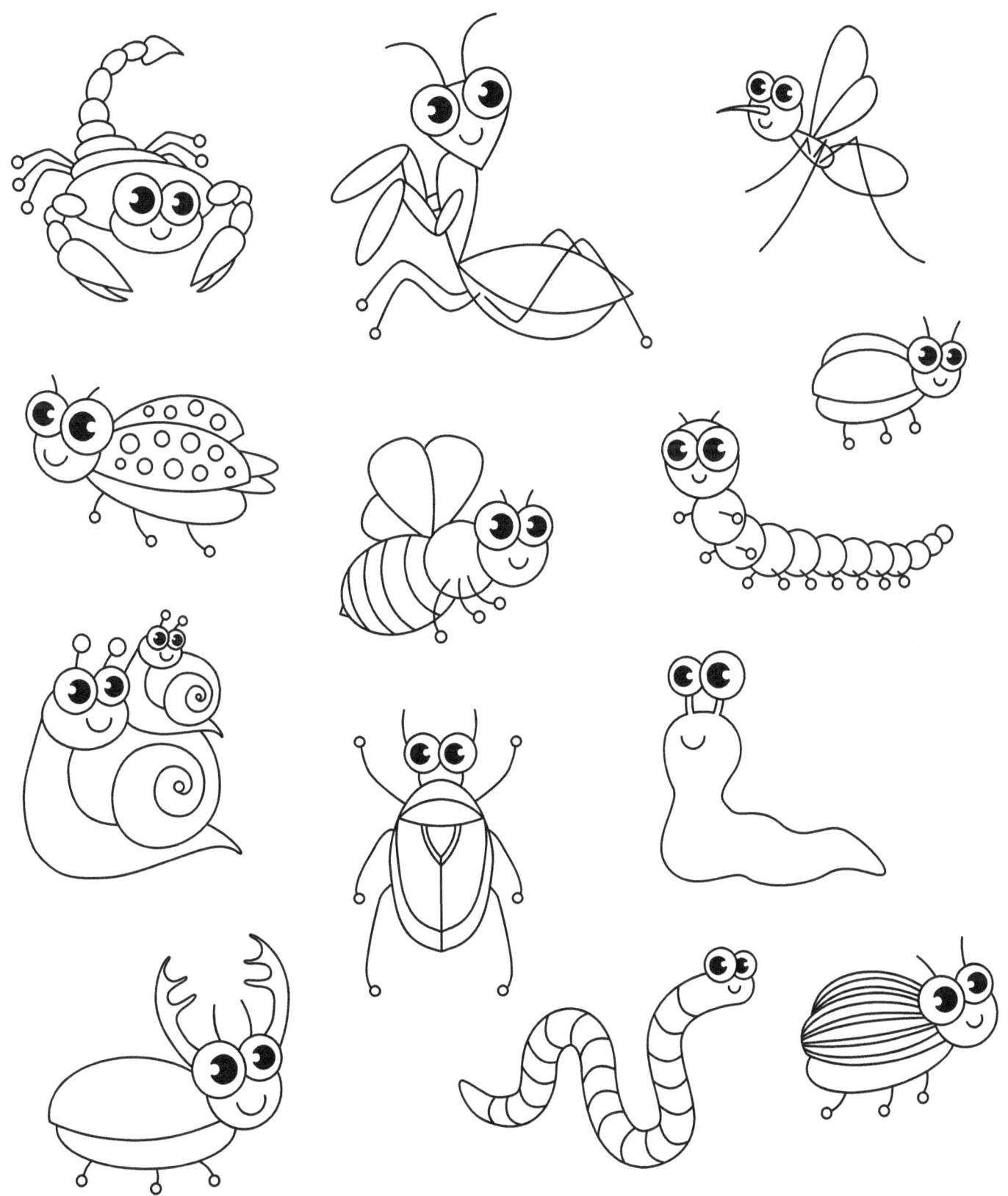

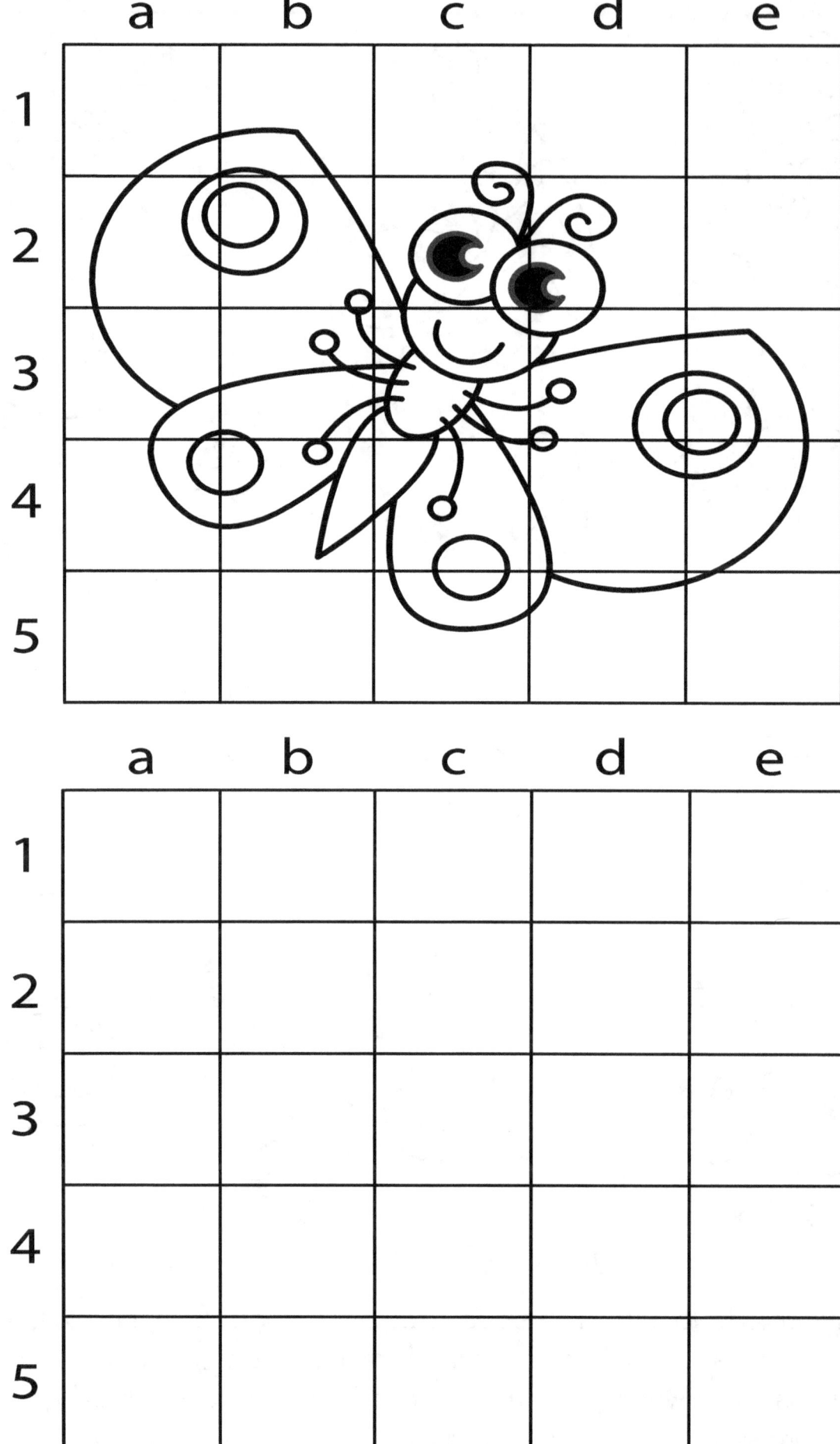

Butterfly

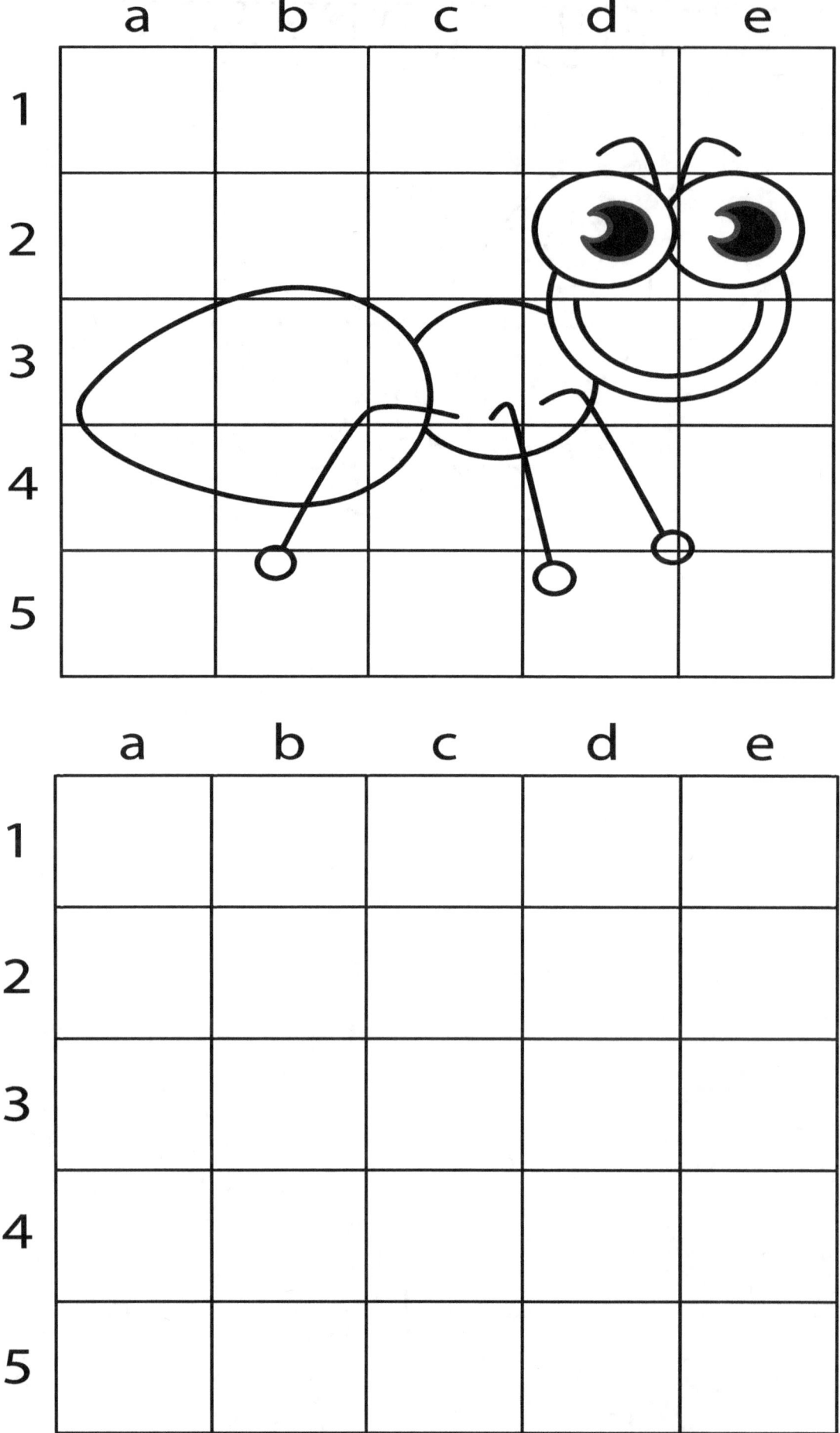

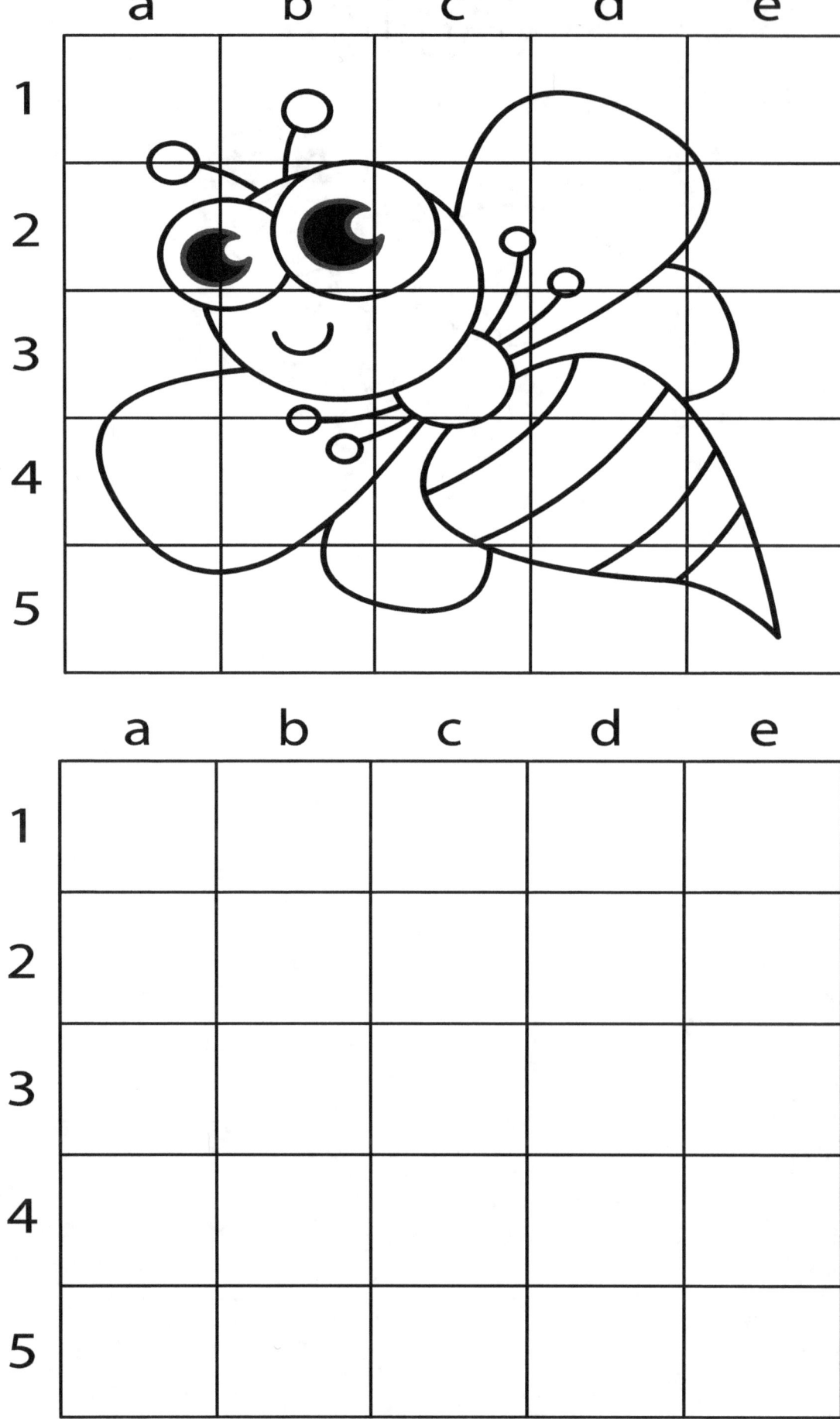

Wasp

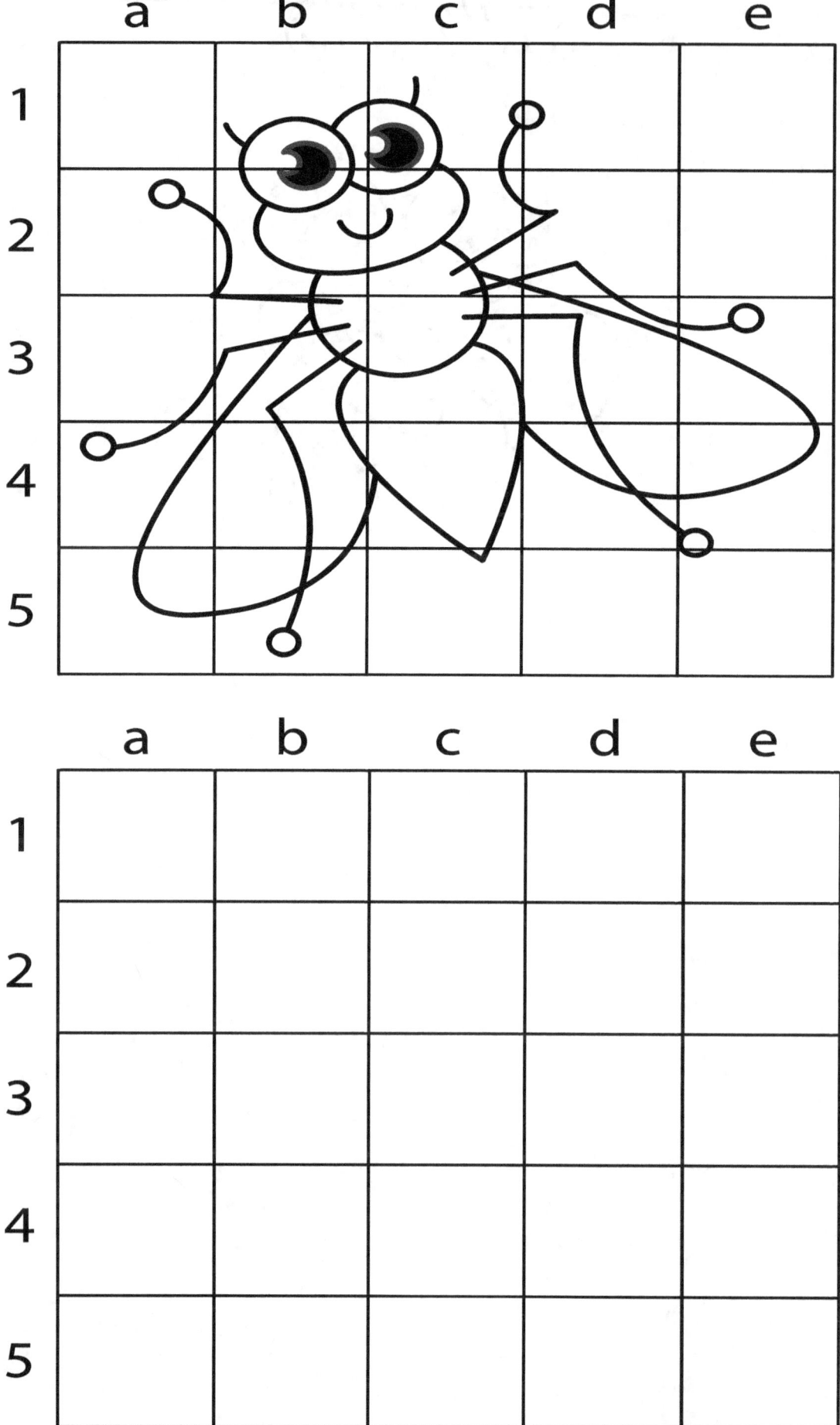

Fly

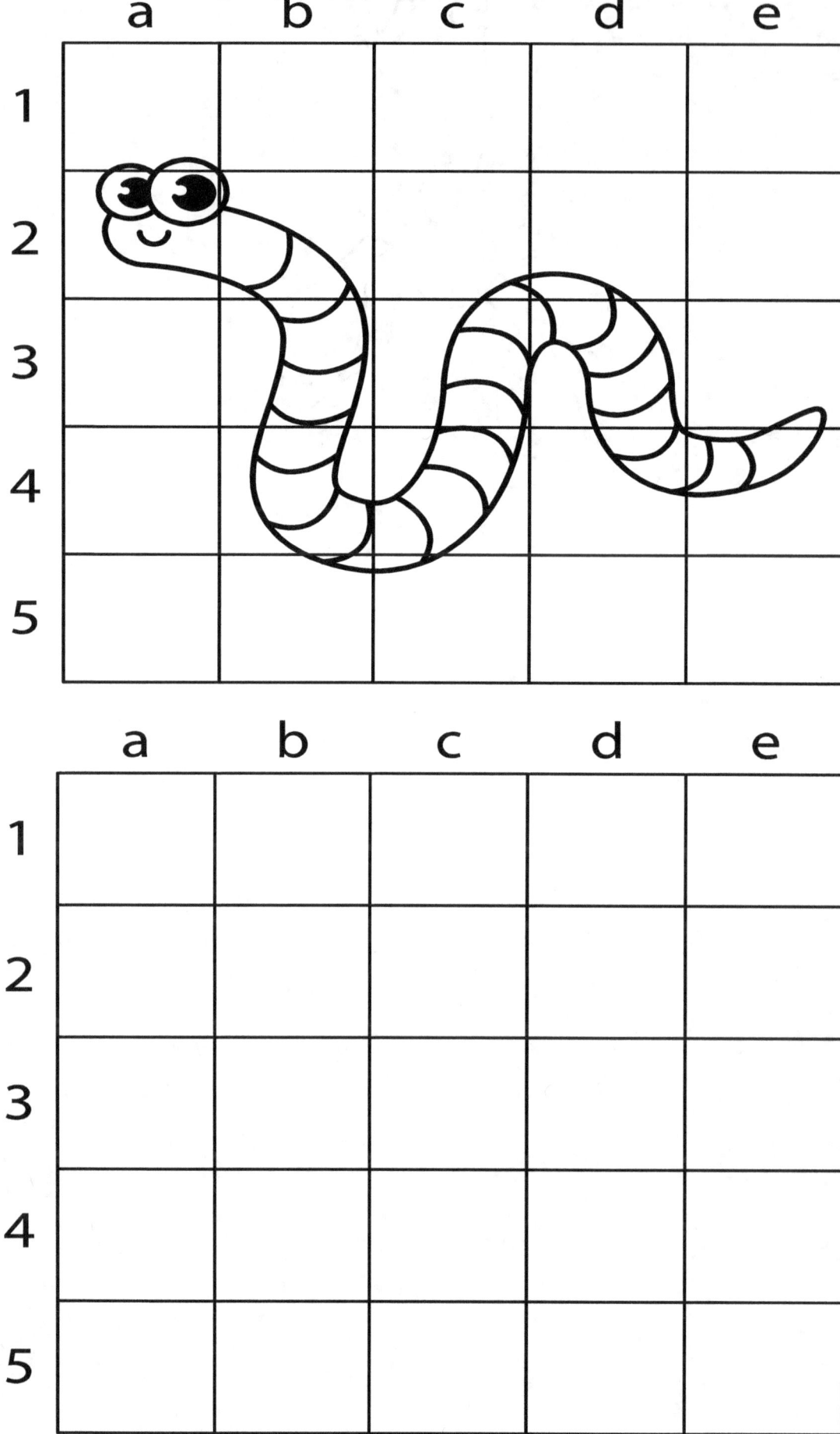

Worm

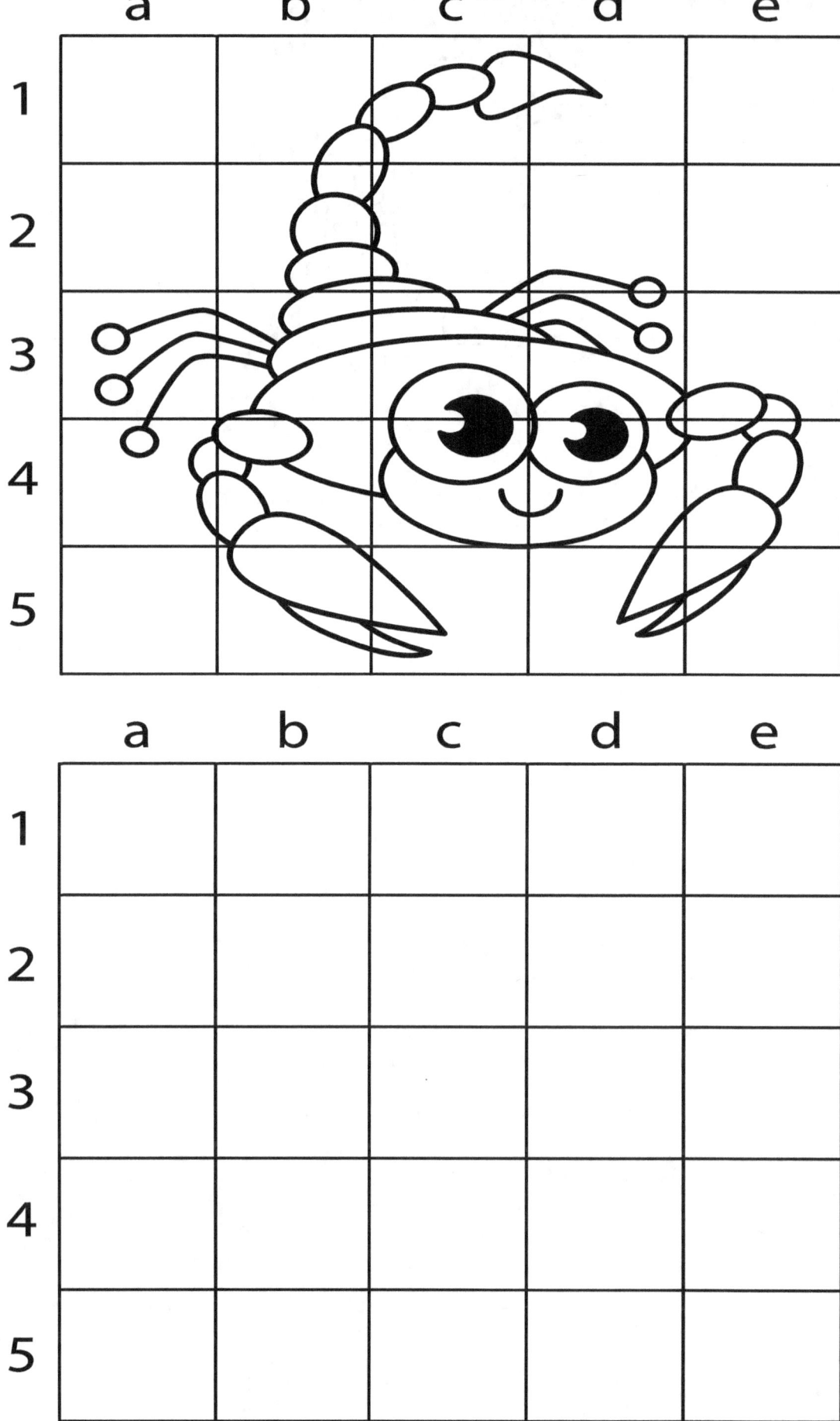

Scorpion

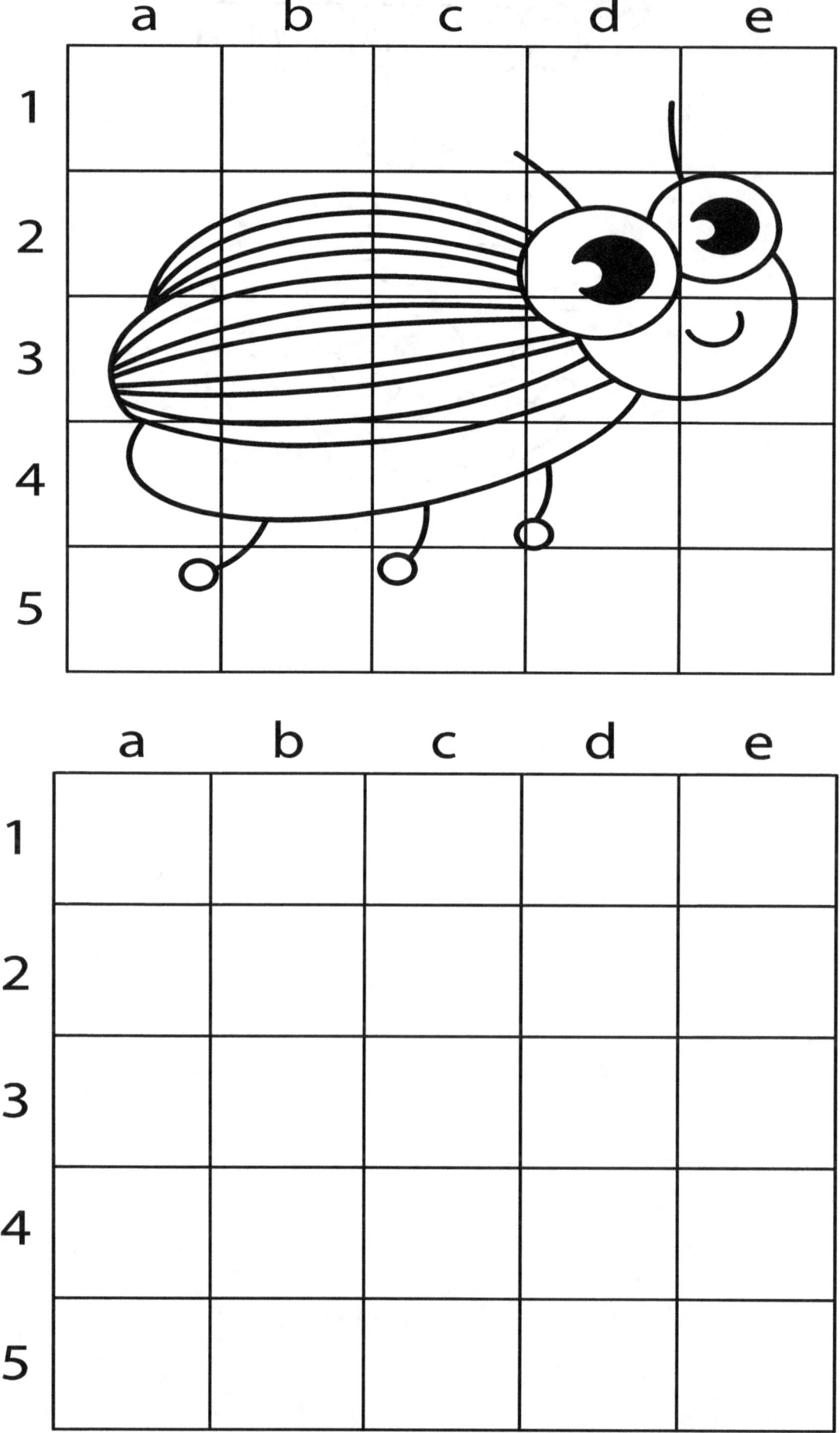

Potato Bug

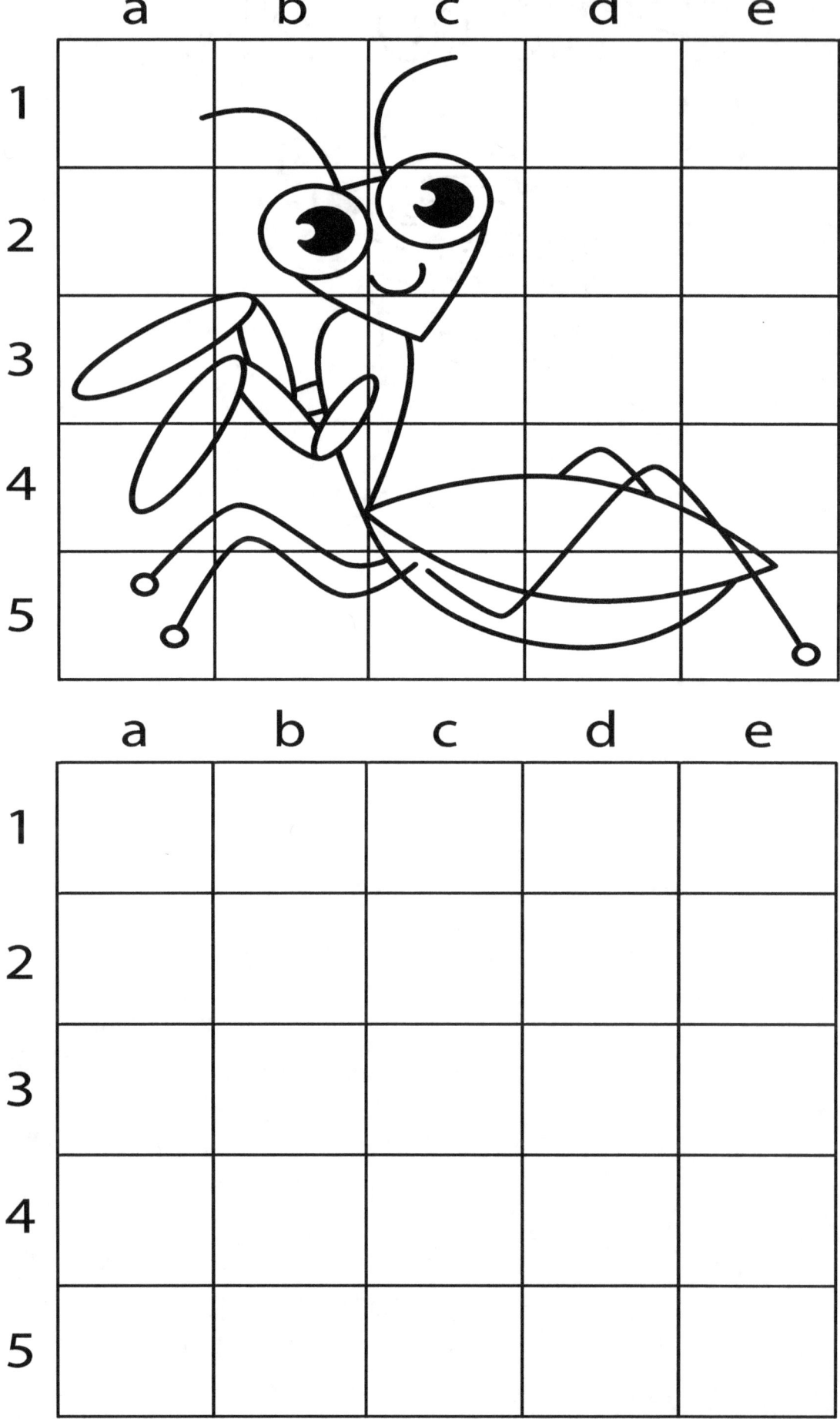

Mantis

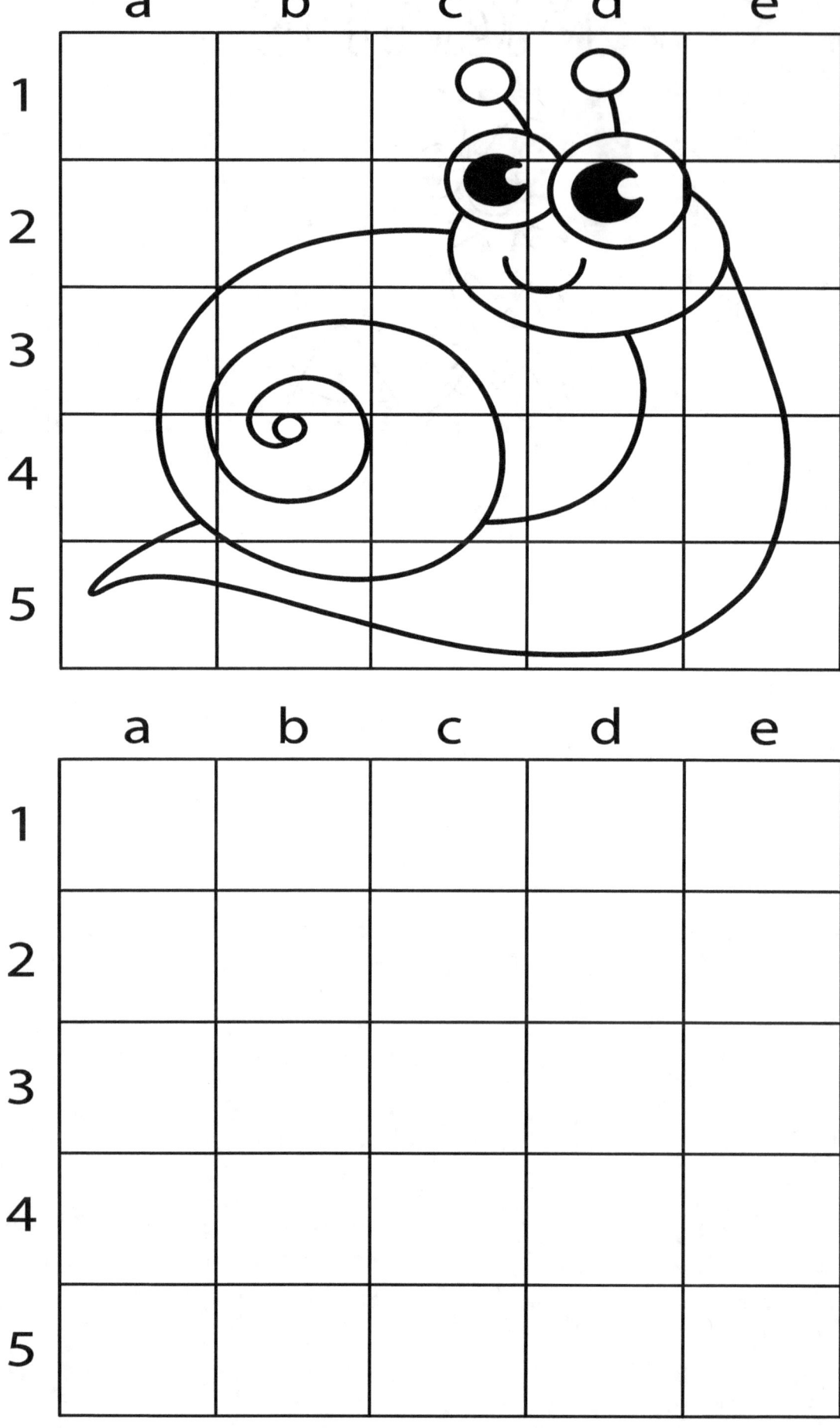

Snail

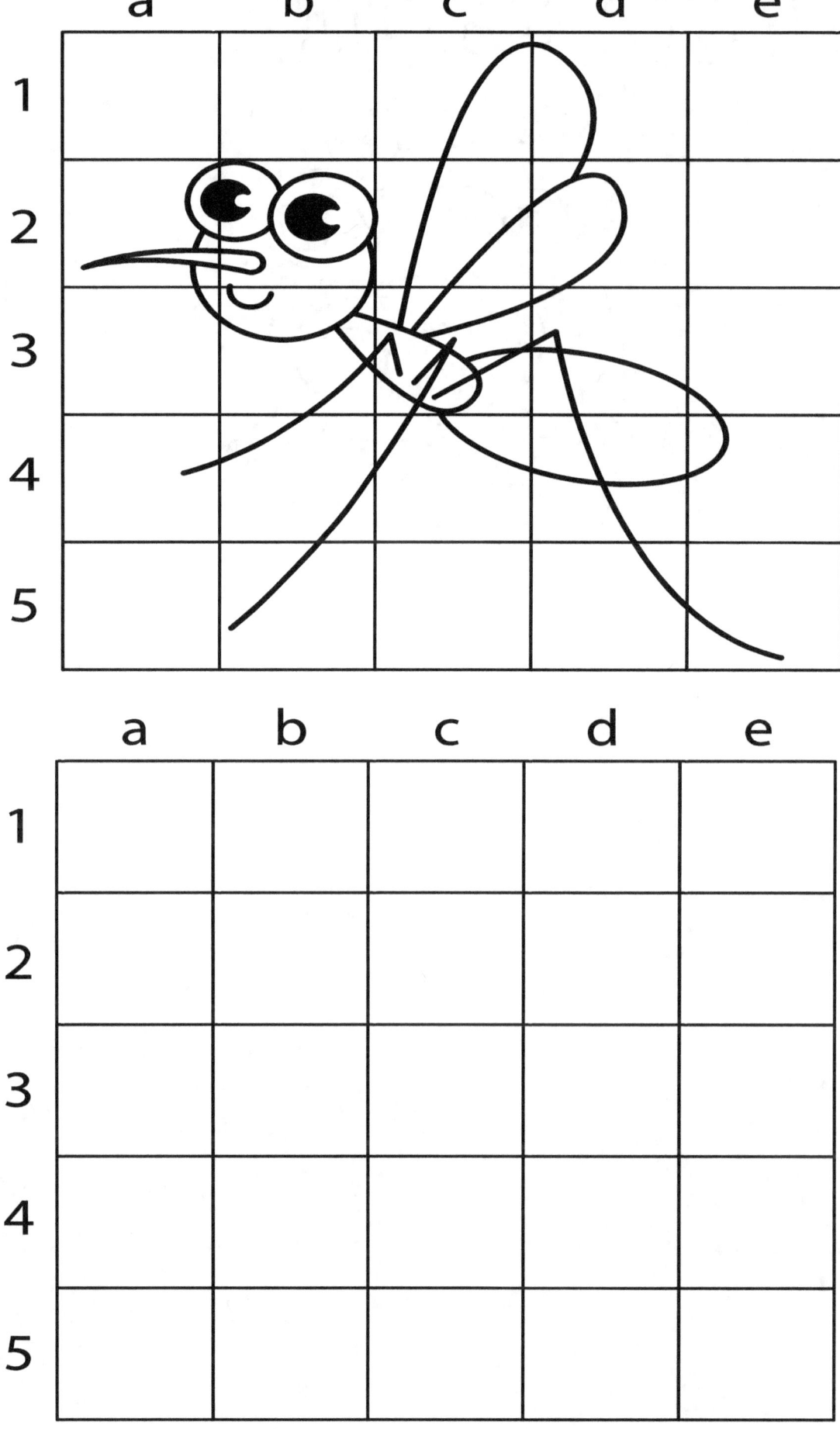

Mosquito

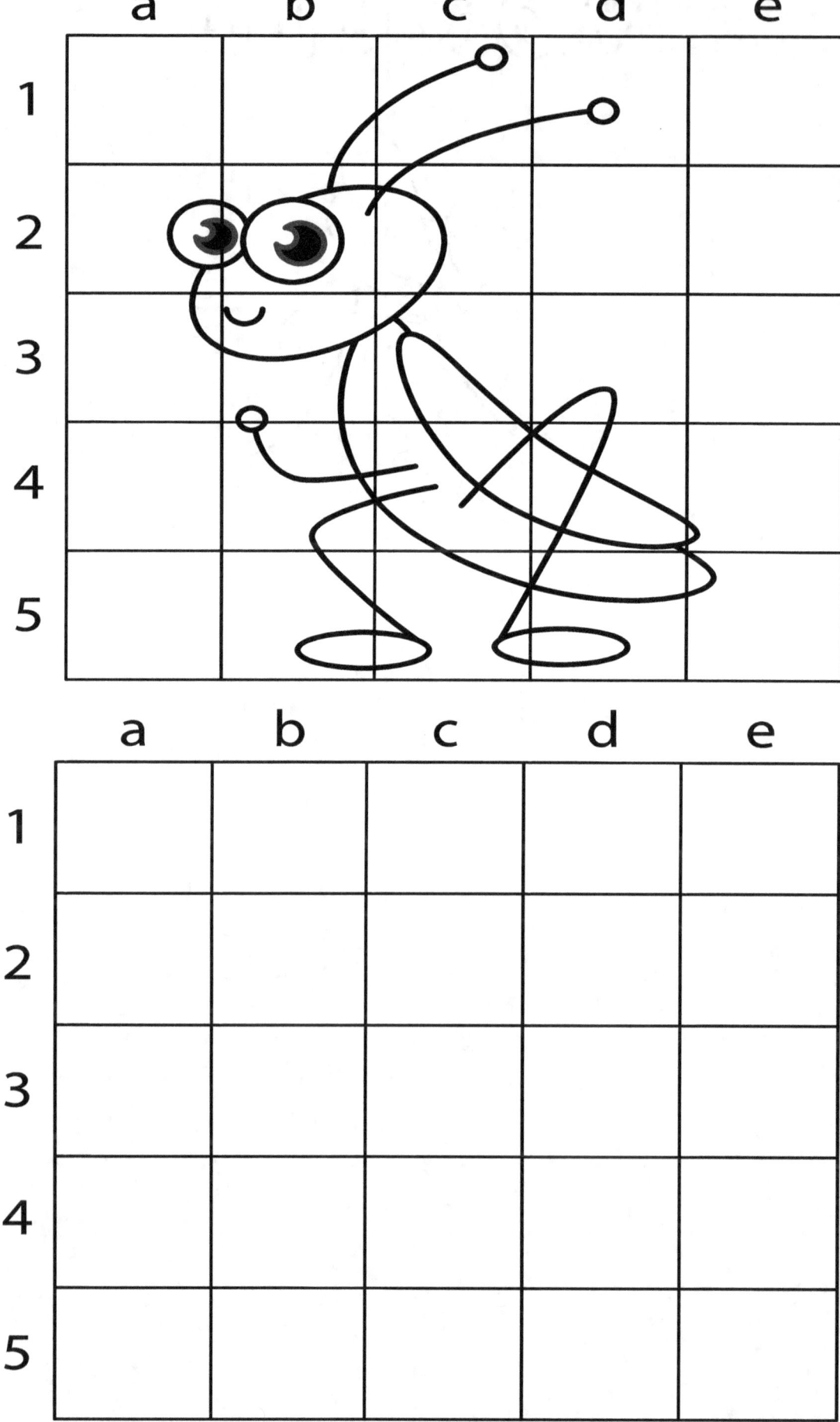

Grasshopper

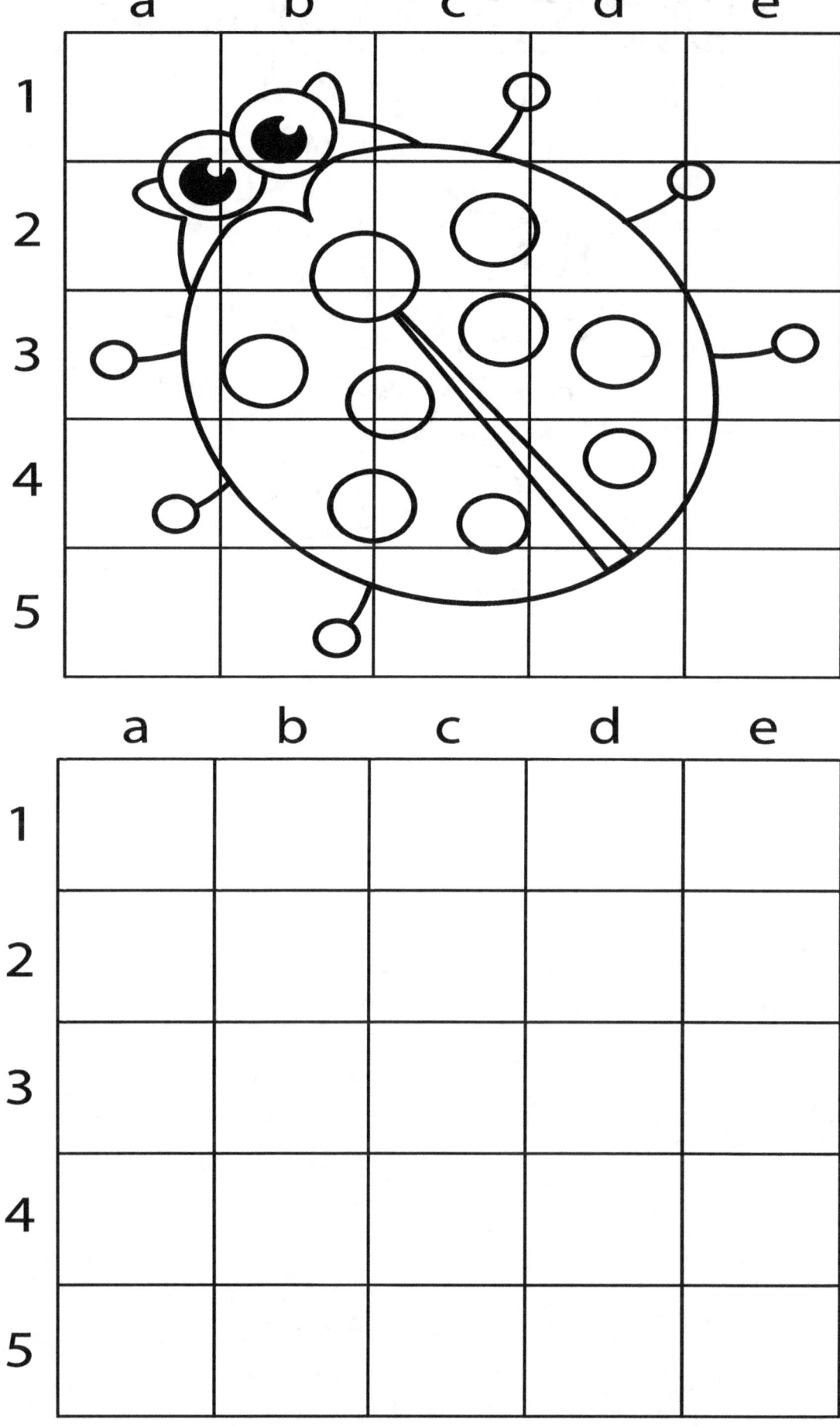

Ladybug

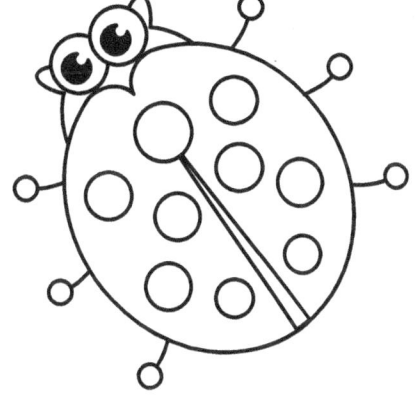

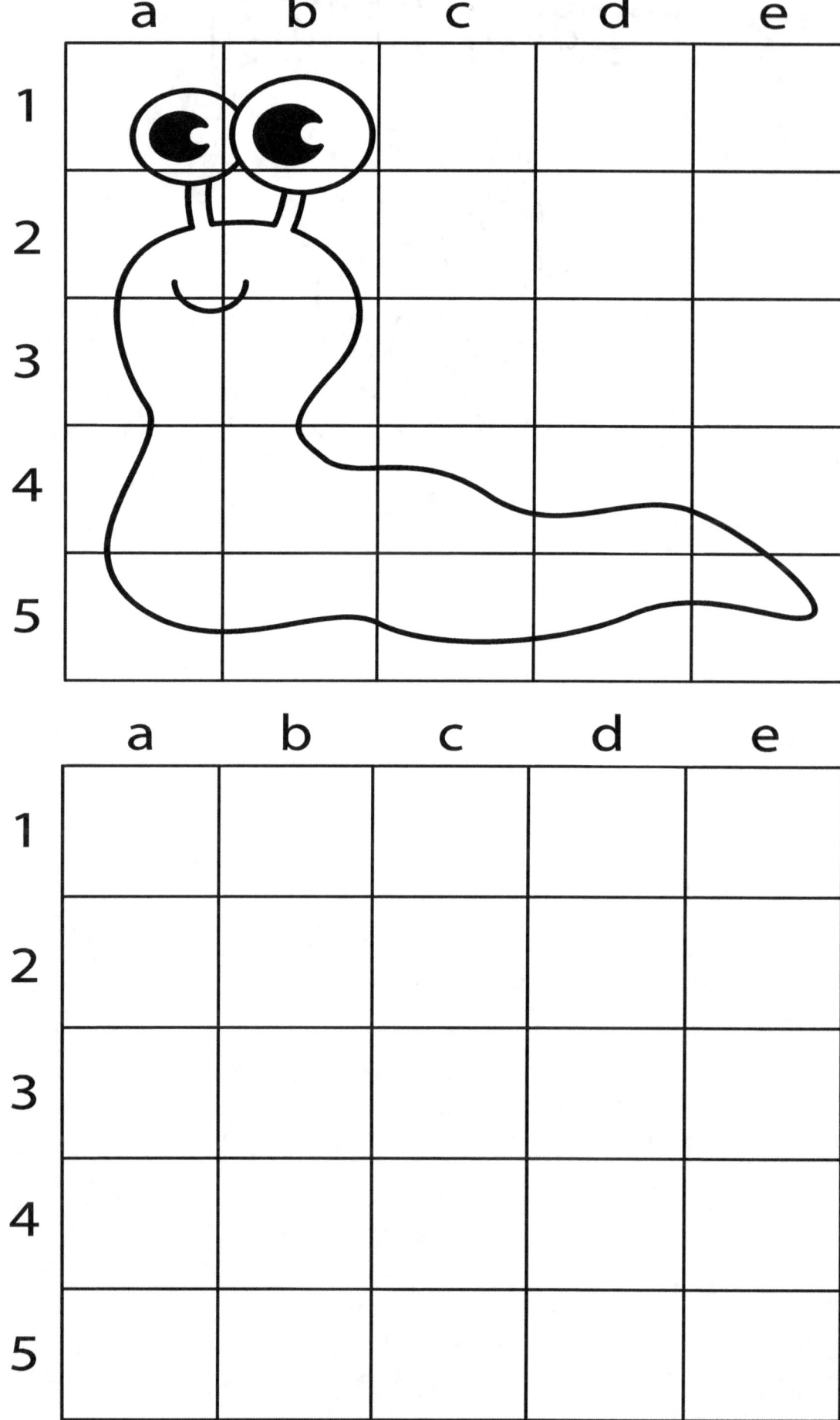

Slug

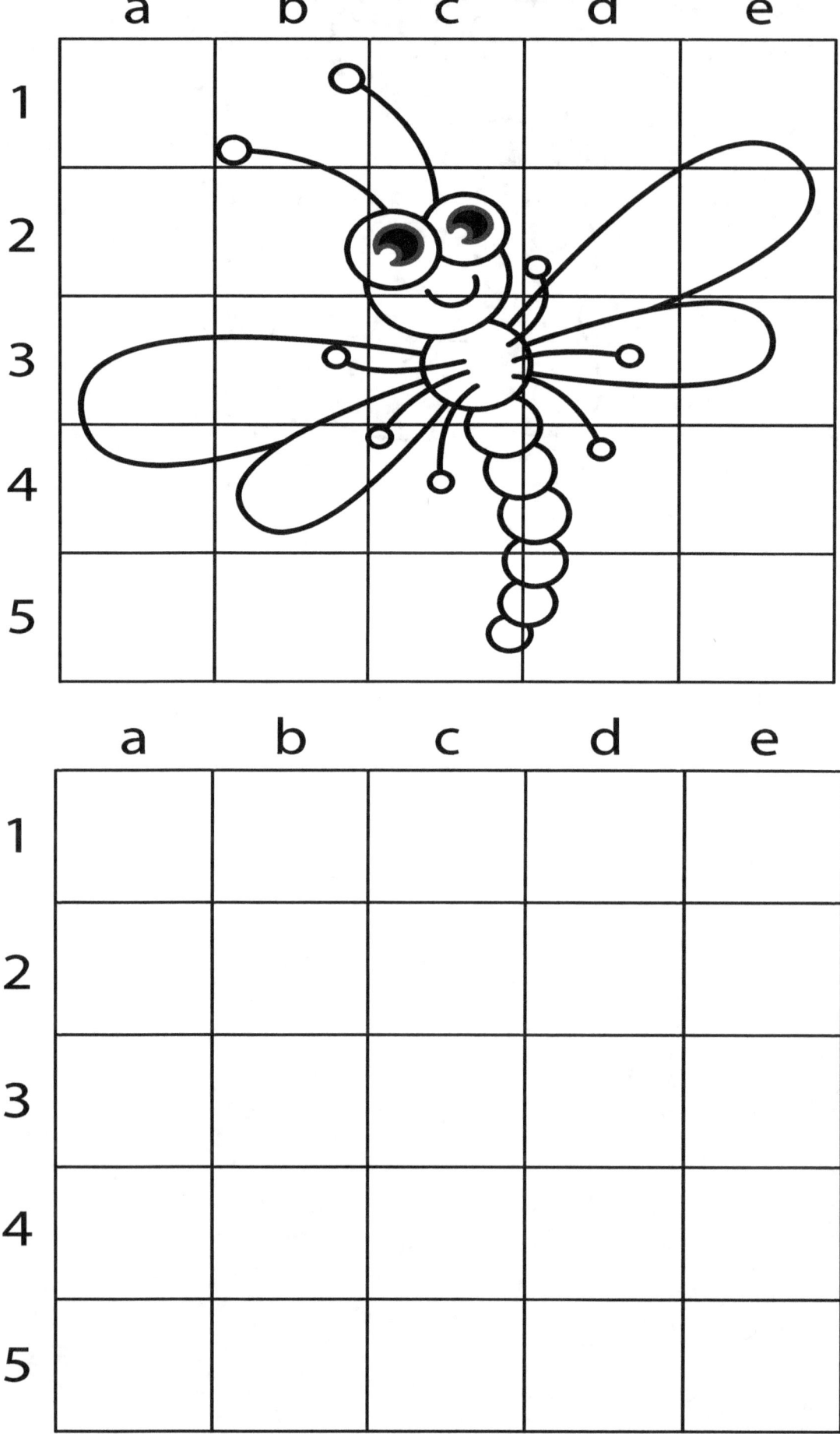

Dragonfly

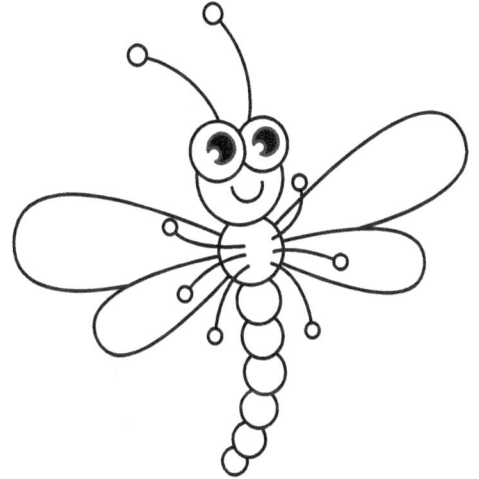

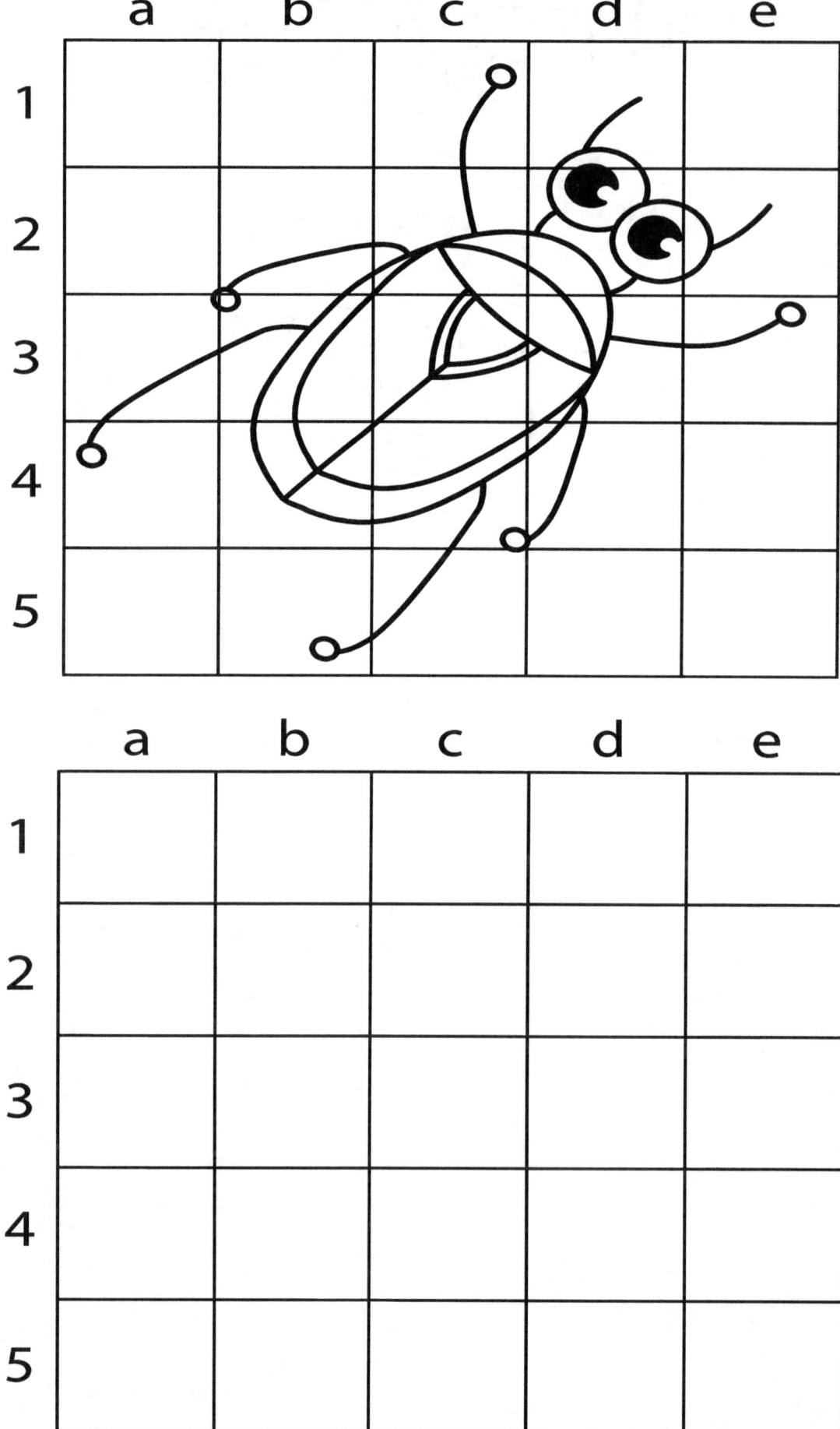

June Bug

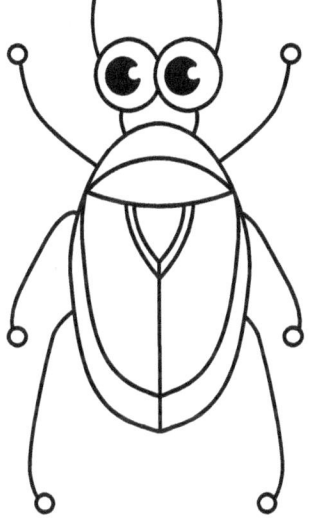

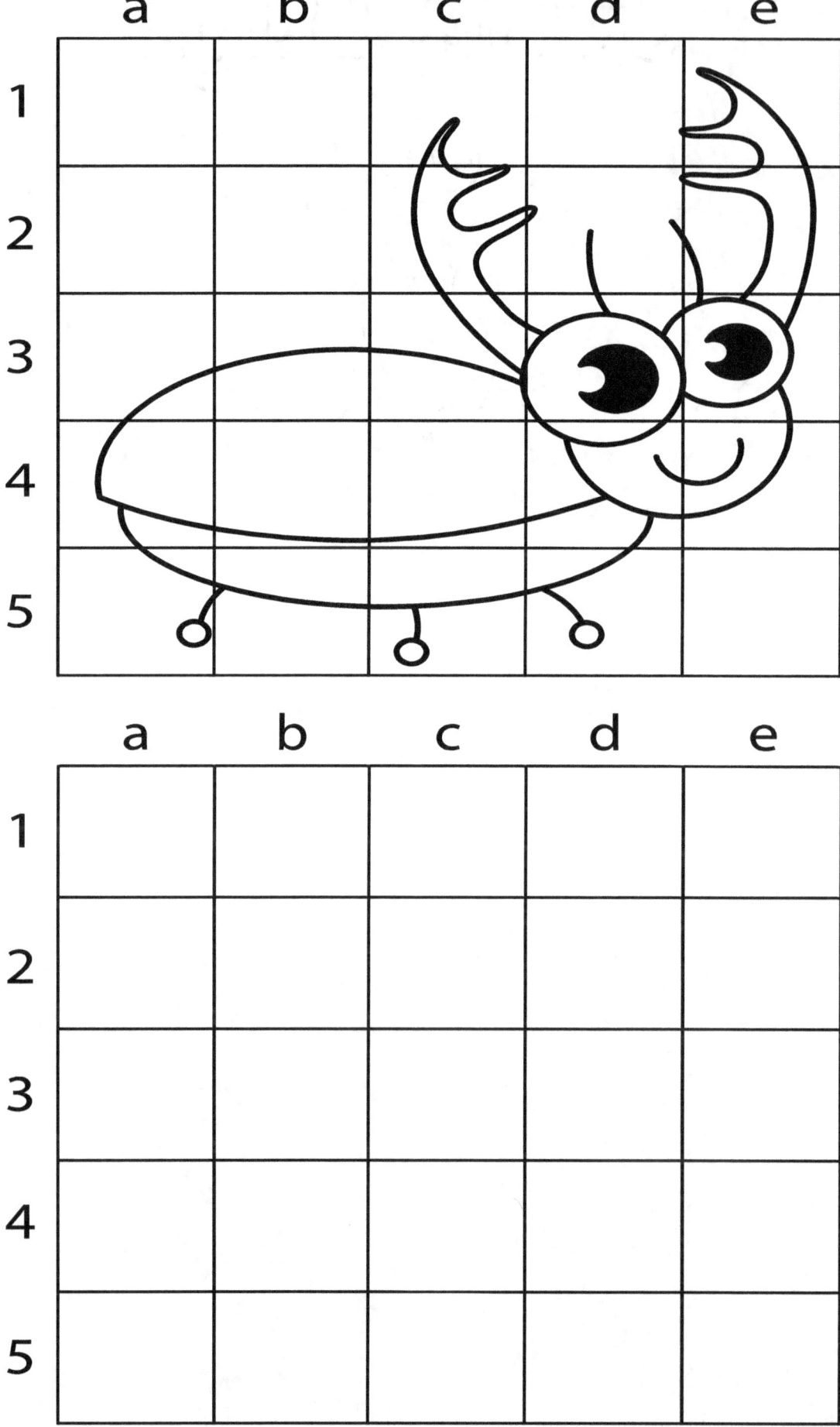

Corn Beetle

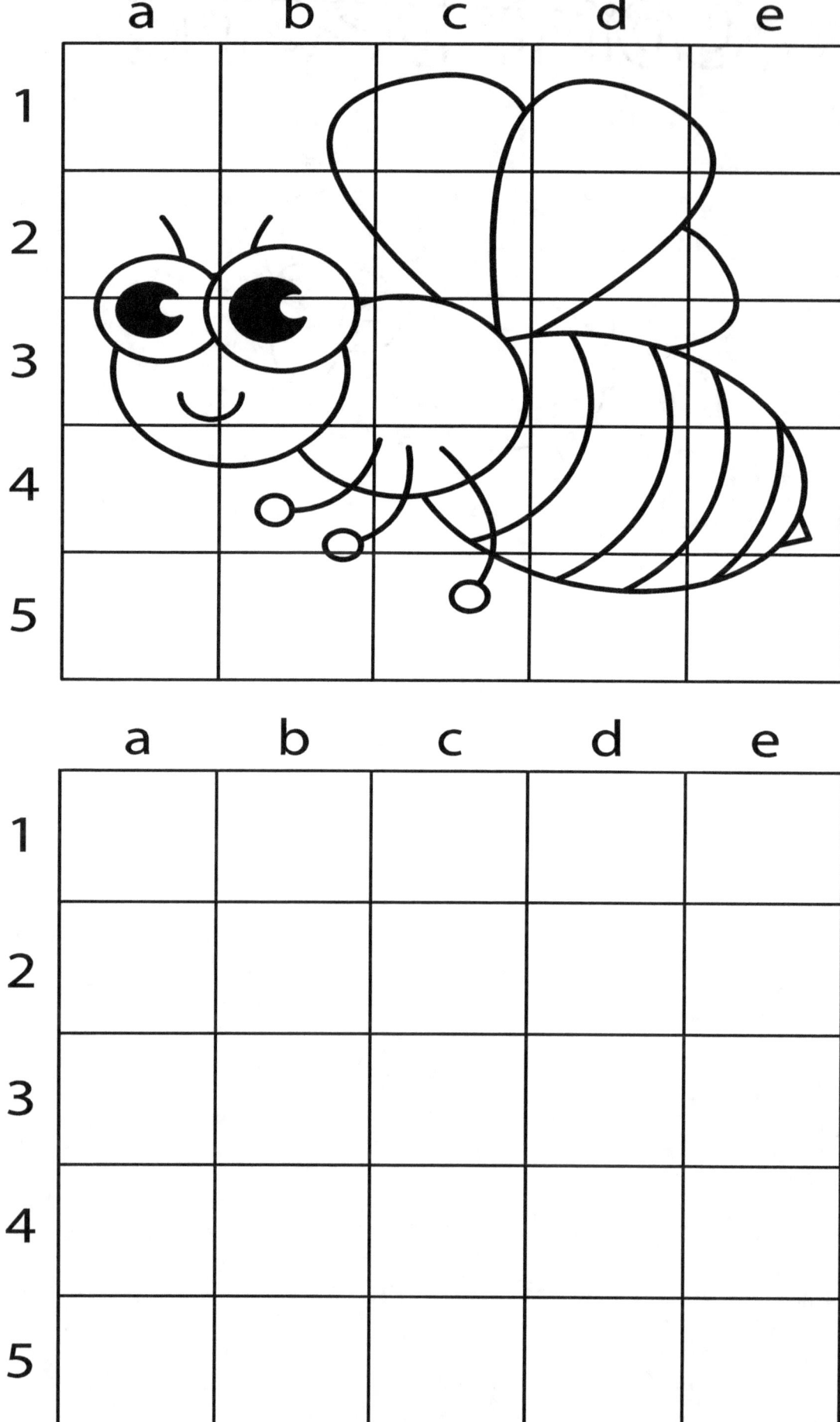

Bee

adventurelearningpress.com